THE JESUS LIFESTYLE

SERIES THREE

NICKY GUMBEL

Published by Alpha International

HTB Brompton Road, London SW7 1JA

publications@alpha.org

CONTENTS

Therefore I tell you, do not worry about your life, what you will eat or drink; or about your body, what you will wear. Is not life more important than food, and the body more important than clothes? Look at the birds of the air; they do not sow or reap or store away in barns, and yet your heavenly Father feeds them. Are you not much more valuable than they? Who of you by worrying can add a single hour to his life?

And why do you worry about clothes? See how the lilies of the field grow. They do not labor or spin. Yet I tell you that not even Solomon in all his splendor was dressed like one of these. If that is how God clothes the grass of the field, which is here today and tomorrow is thrown into the fire, will he not much more clothe you, O you of little faith? So do not worry, saying, 'What shall we eat?' or 'What shall we drink?' or 'What shall we wear?' For the pagans run after all these things, and your heavenly Father knows that you need them. But seek first his kingdom and his righteousness, and all these things will be given to you as well. Therefore do not worry about tomorrow, for tomorrow will worry about itself. Each day has enough trouble of its own.

MATTHEW
6:25–34

how to **stop** worrying and **start living**

INTRODUCTION

Jesus never said, 'Don't worry, because there won't be anything to worry about.'

He himself had plenty to worry about: bereavement, temptation, extreme pain, and the responsibility of the salvation of the world.

Jesus encouraged us not to worry, *in spite of* the fact there is so much to worry about.

He offers us six practical steps to cope with worry.

1 UNDERSTAND LIFE'S PURPOSE

2 KEEP PERSPECTIVE

❝Therefore I tell you, do not worry about your life, what you will eat or drink; or about your body, what you will wear. Is not life more important than food, and the body more important than clothes?❞

MATTHEW 6:25

Life is far more important than material things. Often our worries are about relatively unimportant things, such as food, drink, and clothing.

If we simply seek these material things, we are missing the whole point of life.

The point of life is a relationship with God.

❝For what shall it profit a man, if he shall gain the whole world, and lose his own soul?❞

MARK 8:36 (AKJV)

❝Look at the birds of the air; they do not sow or reap or store away in barns, and yet your heavenly Father feeds them. Are you not much more valuable than they?❞

MATTHEW 6:26

Worry is illogical, because it suggests God is more interested in his pets than his children!

Our father in heaven loves us so much he sent his only son to die for us.

We can feel secure in God's love: we need not be afraid, we need not worry.

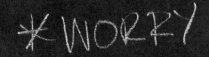

2 KEEP PERSPECTIVE (CONTINUED)

3 BE PRACTICAL

> **The Lord is my shepherd, I shall not be in want ...**
> **Even though I walk**
> **Through the valley of the shadow of death,**
> **I will fear no evil, for you are with me;**
> **Your rod and your staff,**
> **They comfort me.**

PSALM 23:1,4

When going though difficult times we should remember that God is ultimately in control; he is the Sovereign Lord.

> **And we know that in all things God works for the good of those who love him, who have been called according to his purpose.**

ROMANS 8:28

> **Who of you by worrying can add a single hour to his life?**

MATTHEW 6:27

Worrying is a complete waste of time. It's futile, unproductive and pointless.

Being practical means looking after ourselves; watching what we eat and drink, making sure we get enough sleep, and taking exercise.

Paul says, **For physical training is of some value, but godliness has value for all things, holding promise for both the present life and the life to come.**

1 TIMOTHY 4:8

> **When I look back on all these worries, I remember the story of an old man who said on his death bed that he had had a lot of trouble in his life, most of which never happened.**

Winston Churchill

#WORRY

4 TRUST GOD'S PROVISION

> **" And why do you worry about clothes? See how the lilies of the field grow. They do not labour or spin. Yet I tell you that not even Solomon in all his splendour was dressed like one of these. If that is how God clothes the grass of the field, which is here today and tomorrow is thrown into the fire, will he not much more clothe you, O you of little faith? So do not worry, saying, 'What shall we eat?' or 'What shall we drink?' or 'What shall we wear?' For the pagans run after all these things, and your heavenly Father knows that you need them. "**

MATTHEW 6:28–32

Faith and anxiety are like fire and water – they do not mix.

Faith involves trust in God's care and provision. We should draw near to God.

In times of anxiety, pick up the Bible.

> **" When anxiety was great within me, your consolation brought joy to my soul. "**

PSALM 94:19

> **" Cast all your anxiety on him because he cares for you. "**

1 PETER 5:7

> **" Do not be anxious about anything, but in everything, by prayer and petition, with thanksgiving, present your requests to God. "**

PHILIPPIANS 4:6

We can also turn to our brothers and sisters in Christ. Paul advised the Galatians to **" carry each other's burdens "**.

GALATIANS 6:2

Sharing our anxieties with others helps us not to become isolated.

* WORRY

NOTES

5 FOCUS ON THE PRESENT

6 SORT OUT YOUR PRIORITIES

❝ Therefore do not worry about tomorrow, for tomorrow will worry about itself. Each day has enough trouble of its own. ❞

MATTHEW 6:34

We will never get rid of all our troubles. Jesus doesn't say that we shouldn't think about the future or plan ahead.

However, he reminds us to focus on the present.

❝ WORRY DOES NOT EMPTY TOMORROW OF SORROW, IT EMPTIES TODAY OF STRENGTH. ❞

Corrie Ten Boom

We should live one day at a time.

❝ But seek first his kingdom and his righteousness, and all these things will be given to you as well. ❞

MATTHEW 6:33

Worry is unnecessary.

Seeking first God's kingdom means getting our priorities right.

Some of our worries are modest – food, drink, and clothes. Others are more grandiose – a bigger house, a new car, a bigger salary, fame, power. These are self-centered and meaningless.

Jesus calls us to take on a different set of responsibilities and a nobler ambition: to seek first his kingdom.

We should seek God's rule and reign in our lives, our marriages, our home, family and lifestyle.

We must also seek God's 'righteousness' in our lives and in society.

ONCLUSION

We need to make the most of our time, energy and money. **We can all make tomorrow better**.

Do what you can, where you are, with what you have.

RECOMMENDED WEBSITE

www.mindandsoul.info

Mind and Soul is a Christian organisation which explores emotional and mental health issues such as anxiety and depression. It combines both pastoral and medical expertise to help the church face the practical and spiritual challenges of emotional and mental distress.

DISCUSSION QUESTIONS

1. What are the kinds of things that worry you on a day to day basis? Do you think you have the right priorities as laid out by Jesus? How do we decide what's important and what is less so? What deserves our worry and/or consideration, and what can be left for God to resolve?

2. Have you ever experienced severe anxiety? What steps did you take/ are you taking to help deal with the problem? How can your experiences help others?

3. Discuss some of the things that Jesus advises us not to worry about: food, drink, clothes (Matthew 6:30). How important are these things to you and your friends?

4. With so much choice, it can be hard not to fall for materialism and consumerism in the 21st century. What measures can we take in order to avoid these temptations? How can we teach others not to place so much importance on material goods?

5. In the Bible, we read: 'If that is how God clothes the grass of the field, which is here today and tomorrow is thrown into the fire, will he not much more clothe you, O you of little faith?' (Matthew 6:30). Is it difficult to trust God's provision? Have you ever had to rely solely on God for your needs? Do you think you could?

6. How can we help to make tomorrow better for ourselves and for others?

Do not judge, or you too will be judged. For in the same way you judge others, you will be judged, and with the measure you use, it will be measured to you.

Why do you look at the speck of sawdust in your brother's eye and pay no attention to the plank in your own eye? How can you say to your brother, 'Let me take the speck out of your eye', when all the time there is a plank in your own eye? You hypocrite, first take the plank out of your own eye, and then you will see clearly to remove the speck from your brother's eye.

Do not give dogs what is sacred; do not throw your pearls to pigs. If you do, they may trample them under their feet, and then turn and tear you to pieces.

MATTHEW 7:1–6

how to **deal** with
criticism

INTRODUCTION

All of us can be on the receiving end of criticism from time to time.

We can never be immune to criticism; we need soft hearts.

When we are criticised, how do we cope with it? How do we react?

What's the difference between **constructive** and **destructive criticism?**

Is it ever right to criticise someone?

What does Jesus say on this subject?

1

DISTINGUISH GOOD JUDGMENT FROM JUDGMENTALISM

❝ Do not judge, or you too will be judged. **❞**

MATTHEW 7:1

We must consider these words in the context of Jesus' teaching as a whole and in the context of the rest of the Bible.

We need judges who can exercise authority in the courts. Discipline is also necessary in the church and in the home. As individual Christians we need to exercise judgment.

We live in a highly critical society. We must stop judging by mere appearances and make right judgments.

❝ Do not give dogs what is sacred; do not throw your pearls to pigs. If you do, they may trample them under their feet, and then turn and tear you to pieces. **❞**

MATTHEW 7:6

We all have to make value judgments.

Jesus isn't attacking judgment, but judgmentalism.

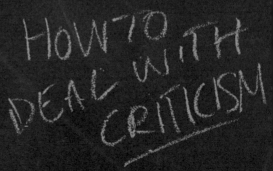

HOW TO DEAL WITH CRITICISM

NOTES

2
TREAT OTHER PEOPLE AS GOD TREATS YOU

3
AVOID FAULT FINDING LIKE THE PLAGUE

❝ Do not judge, or you too will be judged. ❞

MATTHEW 7:1

Treat other people as God treats you.

God has forgiven us so we need not feel judged or condemned.

❝ Do not judge, and you will not be judged. Do not condemn, and you will not be condemned. Forgive, and you will be forgiven. ❞

LUKE 6:37

❝FORGIVENESS IS NOT AN OCCASIONAL ACT, IT IS A PERMANENT ATTITUDE. ❞
Martin Luther King, Jr.

We should cultivate an attitude of generous forgiving. We should overlook people's faults and offences.

❝ Why do you look at the speck of sawdust in someone else's eye and pay no attention to the plank in your own eye ... you hypocrite. ❞

MATTHEW 7:3,5A

Much criticism is blind criticism.

❝ I never found in a long experience of politics that criticism is ever inhibited by ignorance. ❞

Harold Macmillan

Criticism can be blinded by ignorance, misunderstanding, sin and hypocrisy.

The things we criticise in others are often the things we see in ourselves.

Speaking ill of others is a way of dishonestly speaking well of ourselves.

❝ You may find hundreds of faultfinders among professed Christians, but all their criticism will not lead one solitary soul to Christ. ❞

D. L. Moody

HOW TO DEAL WITH CRITICISM

NOTES

4 WELCOME CONSTRUCTIVE CRITICISM

5 TRY TO FIND 'A KERNEL OF TRUTH' IN EVERY CRITIC'S ATTACK

❝ ... first take the plank out of your own eye ... ❞

MATTHEW 7:5B

Not all criticism is bad. 'Good' criticism consists of 'analytical evaluation', as exercised by the music, art or film critic. 'Bad' criticism consists of finding fault.

We all need help to get the plank out of our eye, so we can see clearly.

Criticism may be hard to take, but it can be very positive and helpful; it helps us to learn and grow.

❝ A fool spurns his father's discipline, but whoever heeds correction shows prudence. ❞

PROVERBS 15:5

❝ ... then you will see clearly ... ❞

MATTHEW 7:5C

How do we respond when we receive criticism that is not of the constructive variety?

If we want to achieve anything in life, we are bound to receive criticism. Jesus himself was inundated by criticism, and he told his followers to expect the same.

If criticism is destructive, it's best to ignore it. Sometimes we need to stand up to the critic. Sometimes we need to have a conversation.

Generally, we should welcome criticism, and try to find in it a 'kernel of truth' so that we can grow.

HOW TO DEAL WITH CRITICISM

6 LEARN HOW TO CRITIQUE CONSTRUCTIVELY

7 SOW MERCY, KINDNESS AND LOVE

❝ ... then you will see clearly to remove the speck from the other person's eye. **❞**

MATTHEW 7:5C

Removing the speck is a very delicate operation; criticism must be done in a very careful way.

The right motivation is vital; criticism should only be given in the context of unconditional love.

Loving confrontation in private is better than criticising someone behind their back. We should try to be specific and avoid criticising unless we can offer a constructive solution.

HOW TO DEAL WITH CRITICISM

❝ For in the same way as you judge others, you will be judged, and with the measure you use, it will be measured to you. **❞**

MATTHEW 7:2

❝ Give, and it will be given to you. A good measure, pressed down, shaken together and running over, will be poured into your lap. For with the measure you use, it will be measured to you. **❞**

LUKE 6:38

If we sow harsh criticism, we will be judged harshly. We will create a negative environment of judgmentalism, and we will reap the consequences. God is the agent of judgment.

If we choose mercy, we will receive God's mercy.

God has not judged us as we deserve, he has not condemned us. He has set us free.

❝ [His mercies] are new every morning; great is [God's] faithfulness. **❞**

LAMENTATIONS 3:23

ONCLUSION

Our words have the power to affect the course of a person's life.

Whatever we sow, we reap. We have received the seed of the gospel and now it is our turn to plant it – in our family, in our workplace, in our church and in our denomination.

The promise of Jesus is that when we plant the seed, we will have an impact. Ultimately, **we can change the world**.

RECOMMENDED READING LIST

Coping With Criticism
Jamie Buckingham

DISCUSSION QUESTIONS

1. What type of criticism do you have to cope with at work or at home?

2. Have you ever criticised somebody? How did it make you feel? Did it come from a place of unconditional love? How did that person respond?

3. Think of a time when you didn't handle criticism well. Keeping Jesus' teaching on criticism in mind, discuss what you could have done differently.

4. What's the difference between discernment, judgment and judgmentalism? Is it ever appropriate to exercise our judgment? If so, when?

5. We live in a highly judgmental society. How can we respond to our critics in a way that will set a better example for those around us?

6. What does Jesus mean when he says, 'Do not give dogs what is sacred; do not throw your pearls to pigs. If you do, they may trample them under their feet, and then turn and tear you to pieces' (Matthew 7:6)?

NOTES

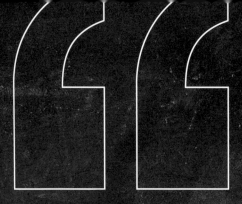

Ask and it will be given to you; seek and you will find; knock and the door will be opened to you. For everyone who asks receives; he who seeks finds; and to him who knocks, the door will be opened.

Which of you, if his son asks for bread, will give him a stone? Or if he asks for a fish, will give him a snake? If you, then, *though you are evil, know how to give good gifts to your children, how much more will your Father in heaven give good gifts to those who ask him! So in everything, do to others what you would have them do to you, for this sums up the Law and the Prophets.*

MATTHEW
7:7–12

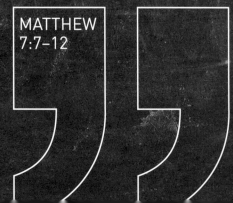

INTRODUCTION

Relationships are a vital aspect of our lives. **Jesus is the relationship expert;** he tells us how to get our relationships right with God and with other people.

Others had taught the negative version of Jesus' teaching: 'What you do not wish to be done to you, do not do to anyone else.' This is the philosophy of the world: 'I don't do anyone any harm; therefore, I lead a good life.'

Jesus redefined goodness when he said, 'Do to others what you to have them do to you.' These are the **most challenging words ever spoken**.

Jesus gives us five practical steps to respond to these words.

1 REACH OUT FOR GOD

2 RELATE TO 'YOUR FATHER'

❝Ask and it will be given to you; seek and you will find; knock and the door will be opened to you. For everyone who asks receives; everyone who seeks finds; and to everyone who knocks, the door will be opened. ❞

MATTHEW 7:7–8

Our purpose is to live in relationship with God.

We must keep on asking, keep on seeking and keep on knocking.

❝ ... your Father in heaven ... ❞

MATTHEW 7:11

There is something very powerful about the relationship between a child and their father. There's something even more powerful about our relationship with the Heavenly Father.

We can love our neighbours because we have a Heavenly Father who loves us.

NOTES

3 RELY ON GOD'S GOODNESS

4 RECEIVE 'GOOD GIFTS'

❝ Which of you, if your children ask for bread, will give them a stone? Or if they ask for a fish, will give them a snake? **❞**

MATTHEW 7:9–10

No human father would be cruel enough to give his child a stone instead of bread or a snake instead of fish.

God would never give us anything harmful; he only gives us good gifts.

❝ If you, then, though you are evil, know how to give good gifts to your children, how much more will your Father in heaven give good gifts to those who ask him! **❞**

MATTHEW 7:11

The Holy Spirit is the greatest of all God's good gifts. God's love is poured into our hearts by the Spirit. It is this experience that enables us to love in the way that Jesus calls us to love.

CHALLENGING WORDS

NOTES

5 RISE TO THE CHALLENGE

CONCLUSIO

❝ So in everything, do to others what you would have them do to you, for this sums up the Law and the Prophets. ❞

MATTHEW 7:12

This is the context of the most challenging words ever spoken. Love is a choice; it is something we can choose to do.

If we love as Jesus tells us to, it will transform all our relationships – our marriages, relationships betweens parents and children and communities.

Jesus pointed to the poor; we can learn from them.

Jesus **redefined goodness** and he himself lived and died in this way. He tells us to **go and do likewise**.

CHALLENGING WORDS

NOTES

DISCUSSION QUESTIONS

1. How many of the five practical steps do you employ in your daily life? What could you do to ensure that you were constantly employing all five?

2. How can we rise to the challenge of 'do[ing] to others what you would have them do to you' (Matthew 7:12)? What opportunities have you had to rise to the challenge?

3. What difference would it make to our society if all Christians lived with these steps in mind all the time?

4. Which of the five practical steps do you find it most easy to implement? Why? How have you demonstrated this particular step recently?

5. Do you find it difficult to live out your faith according to Jesus' words? Which aspects of living counter-culturally do you struggle with?

6. Jesus lived amongst the poor. Why did he choose to do that? What does this teach us?

Independence.

NOTES

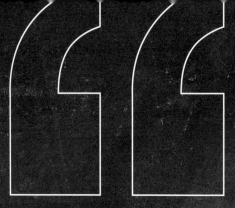

Enter through the narrow gate. For wide is the gate and broad is the road that leads to destruction, and many enter through it. But small is the gate and narrow the road that leads to life, and only a few find it.

MATTHEW
7:13–14

how to **make** the
big decision

INTRODUCTION

> **"Enter through the narrow gate."**
>
> **MATTHEW 7:13**

Jesus has talked about what it means to follow him, and now it's time for the verdict; **the big decision**.

What is Jesus asking us to do?

1 CHOOSE TO LIVE A RADICAL LIFE

2 TAKE THE LONG VIEW

There are two possible lifestyles, two roads we can choose from. One is broad, the other is narrow.

66 Broad is the road. 99

MATTHEW 7:13

66 Narrow is the road. 99

MATTHEW 7:14

The broad road offers a life of ease. There are no boundaries. You need not keep Jesus' standards. People may get hurt.

The narrow road has boundaries – those set out by Jesus in the Sermon on the Mount. Living on this road is counter-cultural: it is a radical way of life, but it is not easy.

We're not alone on the narrow road; Jesus goes with us.

Jesus sets before us two destinations. Where are they leading?

The broad road **66 leads to destruction. 99**

MATTHEW 7:13

The narrow road **66 leads to life. 99**

MATTHEW 7:14

Jesus warns us that the broad road will destroy us. The narrow road is a tough road, but it leads to life.

Greek words for life:

Bios – life in the biological sense

Zoe – spiritual life with God, this starts now and lasts forever

THE BIG DECISION

NOTES

3 ASPIRE TO BE A GOOD ROLE MODEL

4 EMBARK ON A LIFE OF ADVENTURE

Jesus sets before us two groups of people: those on the broad road and those on the narrow road.

There are many people on the broad road:

❝ Many enter through it. ❞

MATTHEW 7:13

There are only a few on the narrow road:

❝ Only a few find it. ❞

MATTHEW 7:14

Despite being 'only a few' there are still many people who are on the narrow road. There are over 2,000 million people who profess the name of Christ.

❝ A great multitude that no one could count, from every nation, tribe, people and language. ❞

REVELATION 7:9

We are in a minority and we may feel alone. In choosing the road that leads to life, we are role models.

How do we get started? Jesus lays before us two entrances, one is wide:

❝ Wide is the gate. ❞

MATTHEW 7:13

One is small:

❝ Small is the gate. ❞

MATTHEW 7:14

The broad road has easy access through a wide gate.

The entrance to the narrow road is small because you can't take the rubbish with you. We need to get rid of the bad stuff.

We have to put our faith in Jesus.

THE BIG DECISION

CONCLUSION

We have to decide which road we want to be on. There is **no middle road**, no third gate.

What do we need to do in order to get on to the narrow road? We have to **repent**, **put our faith in Jesus**, and **receive his Spirit**. We cannot do it without him.

NOTES

DISCUSSION QUESTIONS

1. What is Jesus asking us to do when he tells us to make 'the big decision'? How can we be sure that we make the right choice? What are the things we should consider?

2. Discuss what Jesus means when he says that the broad road 'leads to destruction' (Matthew 7:13) and that the narrow road 'leads to life' (Matthew 7:14).

3. What steps can we take to ensure that we are acting as good role models for the rest of society, including those who are on the 'broad road' (Matthew 7:13)? How can our actions and lives have an impact on the people around us?

4. How does it make you feel to know that when we take the 'narrow road' (Matthew 7:14), Jesus takes the road with us?

5. In order to fit through the small gate, we need to get rid of all the bad stuff in our lives. How can we achieve this? Where do we begin?

6. What experience have you had of being in a Christian minority? How did it feel?

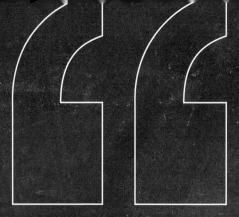

Watch out for false prophets. They come to you in sheep's clothing, but inwardly they are ferocious wolves. By their fruit you will recognise them. Do people pick grapes from thornbushes, or figs from thistles? Likewise every good tree bears good fruit, but a bad tree bears bad fruit. A good tree cannot bear bad fruit, and a bad tree cannot bear good fruit. Every tree that does not bear good fruit is cut down and thrown into the fire. Thus, by their fruit you will recognise them.

Not everyone who says to me, 'Lord, Lord,' will enter the kingdom of heaven, but only he who does the will of my Father who is in heaven. Many will say to me on that day, 'Lord, Lord, did we not prophesy in your name, and in your name drive out demons and perform many miracles?' Then I will tell them plainly, 'I never knew you. Away from me, you evildoers!'

MATTHEW
7:15–23

how to **spot**
false prophets

INTRODUCTION

"Watch out for false prophets ... they are ferocious wolves. "   MATTHEW 7:15

Wolves are a natural enemy of sheep. Jesus wants to **protect his flock**.

How do we **spot false prophets?** How do we distinguish the cults from the church?

"By their fruit you will recognise them. "

MATTHEW 7:16,20

The false prophets will reveal themselves, not by their roots but **by their fruit**.

"Do people pick grapes from thornbushes, or figs from thistles? Likewise every good tree bears good fruit, but a bad tree bears bad fruit. A good tree cannot bear bad fruit, and a bad tree cannot bear good fruit. "

MATTHEW 7:16–18

We need to look closely. What kind of fruit are we looking for?

1

THE FRUIT OF CHARACTER

❝ They come to you in sheep's clothing, but inwardly they are ferocious wolves ... Not everyone who says to me, 'Lord, Lord,' will enter the kingdom of heaven ... Many will say to me on that day, 'Lord, Lord, did we not prophesy in your name, and in your name drive out demons and perform many miracles?' **❞**

MATTHEW 7:15, 21–22

We won't recognise a false prophet by their clothing. They may use Christian language and do things that Christians do, but we must look at the fruit of their character (**MATTHEW 5:1–16**).

If someone has the Holy Spirit inside them, they will produce fruit:

❝ But the fruit of the Spirit is love, joy, peace, patience, kindness, goodness, faithfulness, gentleness and self-control. Against such things there is no law. **❞**

GALATIANS 5:22–23

If we look for the fruit of the Holy Spirit, we will recognise who the false prophets are.

- **Be filled with the Holy Spirit**

FALSE PROPHETS

2 THE FRUIT OF CONDUCT

3 THE FRUIT OF TEACHING

Jesus tells us that those who **" ... do the will of [the] Father ... "** will enter the kingdom of God.

MATTHEW 7:21

To the false prophets, he says, **" Away from me, you evildoers! "**

MATTHEW 7:23

What we believe affects how we live.

We all fail sometimes, but God forgives us.

There's a difference between a person who seeks to live a consistent life and someone who sets out to deceive while disguising themselves as a 'sheep' out of self-interest and self-gain.

Seek to do the will of God, and to make a difference in society.

- **Live a consistent life**

FALSE PROPHETS

What we teach has an impact on people's lives.

" ... a tree is recognised by its fruit ... out of the overflow of the heart the mouth speaks ... For by your words you will be acquitted, and by your words you will be condemned. "

MATTHEW 12:33–37

Deuteronomy gives us a way to test for false prophets:

" If a prophet ... says, 'Let us follow other gods' ... you must not listen to the words of that prophet ... "

DEUTERONOMY 13:1–3

We are to test a person by their teaching. Does their teaching lead us towards God or away from him?

We must check teaching against the Bible.

We don't need to study the counterfeit prophets to know a true one.

- **Soak yourselves in the truth**

4 THE FRUIT OF LOVE

5 THE FRUIT OF RELATIONSHIP

Love and fruitfulness go hand in hand.

❝ I am the vine; you are the branches. If you remain in me and I in you, you will bear much fruit ... This is to my Father's glory, that you bear much fruit, showing yourselves to be my disciples. As the Father has loved me, so have I loved you. Now remain in my love. ❞

JOHN 15:5-9

❝ Do not judge, or you too will be judged. ❞

MATTHEW 7:1

- Love is the first fruit of the Holy Spirit; it encompasses the others

- Love embraces all parts of the church

- Love submits to authority

- Love allows freedom

- **Always act in love**

Without a relationship with God, we can't do anything of any real value. If we abide in him, we will bear much fruit.

Jesus never knew the false prophets; he was never in real relationship with them.

❝ ... I never knew you. ❞

MATTHEW 7:23

There are three tests in the Old Testament that help you check for a false prophet:

1. Their teaching
2. Do their prophesies come true?
3. Have they stood in the council of the Lord?

❝ But which of them has stood in the council of the Lord to see or to hear his word? ... if they had stood in my council, they would have proclaimed my words to my people ... ❞

JEREMIAH 23:18-22

- **Stay close to Jesus**

FALSE PROPHETS

6

THE FRUIT OF INFLUENCE

CONCLUSIO

What is the fruit of the ministry? What is the ministry's impact on other people's lives? Is it producing a community united in love? Is it producing people who live in the way Jesus has taught?

" ... everyone who is fully trained will be like their teacher. **"**

LUKE 6:40

What is the long-term influence of the ministry? The test of deep teaching is the influence on people's lives.

" But everyone who prophesies speaks to people for their strengthening, encouragement and comfort. **"**

1 CORINTHIANS 14:3

- **Look at the long-term**

FALSE PROPHETS

p.054

Watch out for **false prophets**, but **be inspired** by the **true prophets**.

DISCUSSION QUESTIONS

1. What are the key dangers of listening to false prophets?

2. When Jesus talks about recognising both true and false prophets by their 'fruit', what does he mean? What kind of fruit are we looking for?

3. What does it mean to 'live a consistent life'? How can we achieve this? What is the importance of consistency?

4. The Old Testament sets out three ways to test for false prophets. What are they, and how can we put them into practice?

5. How can we be sure whether or not someone has a living relationship with Jesus Christ?

6. Have you ever come into contact with a false prophet? How did you know? What was your experience?

NOTES

'Therefore everyone who hears these words of mine and puts them into practice is like a wise man who built his house on the rock. The rain came down, the streams rose, and the winds blew and beat against that house; yet it did not fall, because it had its foundation on the rock. But everyone who hears these words of mine and does not put them into practice is like a foolish man who built his house on sand. The rain came down, the streams rose, and the winds blew and beat against that house, and it fell with a great crash.'

When Jesus had finished saying these things, the crowds were amazed at his teaching, because he taught as one who had authority, and not as their teachers of the law.

MATTHEW 7:24–29

how to **build** a
secure future

INTRODUCTION

People want to know what the future holds for them.

**❝ ... everyone who hears these words of mine
and puts them into practice is like a wise man
who built his house on the rock ... ❞**

MATTHEW 7:24,26

Jesus tells us how to build a **secure future**.

There is a difference between hearing the words
of Jesus and putting them **into practice**.

Jesus gives an illustration: there are two men,
two houses, two foundations, two results and two
responses.

1 BE PREPARED FOR STORMS

2 THINK

❝The rain came down, the streams rose, and the winds blew and beat against that house ... The rain came down, the streams rose, and the winds blew and beat against that house ...❞

MATTHEW 7:25,27

Be prepared for the challenges of life.

Both the wise man and the foolish man built houses. Superficially, the houses seem to be the same. But we discover the difference when the challenge comes.

Our lives are like houses – their significance is for all eternity.

The challenges of life come in many forms – misunderstandings, disappointments, pressures, sickness, bereavement, tragedy, persecution, failure. And we will all face judgment.

Jesus tells us that we don't need to be afraid – our houses will stand. It is possible to know that our future is secure.

❝... like a wise man ...❞

MATTHEW 7:24

❝... like a foolish man ...❞

MATTHEW 7:26

The foolish person doesn't think.

Don't be a fool, don't miss out on all the amazing things that God has for your life.

Either we are wise, or foolish – there is no 'third building'.

BUILDING A SECURE FUTURE

3 BUILD STRONG FOUNDATIONS

4 CONSIDER THE LONG-TERM

❝ ... it did not fall, because it had its foundation on the rock. ❞

MATTHEW 7:25

❝ ... dug down deep and laid the foundation on rock. ❞

LUKE 6:48

The wise man built his house **❝ on rock ❞**; the foolish man built his **❝ on sand ❞**. The wise man **❝ dug down deep ❞**.

LUKE 6:48

The fool doesn't think about the foundational questions:

- Why are we here?

- What is the meaning of life?

- What is the ultimate purpose of life?

Until we know the purpose of life, we cannot tell what we should be doing with our life.

God's purpose for us is to be living in a relationship with him. When we've sorted that out, everything else takes its place.

Because the foundations of each house were different, the result of the storm was very different for each:

The wise man's house **❝ did not fall. ❞**

MATTHEW 7:25

The foolish man's house **❝ fell with a great crash. ❞**

MATTHEW 7:27

Jesus is warning us out of love. He doesn't want us to get hurt.

The wise man's house withstood the storms, and lasted into eternity.

BUILDING A SECURE FUTURE

5 TAKE ACTION

6 RESPOND TO JESUS

66 ... puts them into practice ... **99**
MATTHEW 7:24

66 ... does not put them into practice ... **99**
LUKE 6:48

This is the key difference. Only one man put the words of Jesus into action.

It's not enough to know about Jesus and hear his words; it's not enough to admire him.

There's a difference between an admirer and a follower.

Jesus is calling followers who will put his words into practice.

God wants us to be the salt and light of the world in order to change the world around us.

66 ... these words of mine ... **99**
MATTHEW 7:24,26

66 ... Jesus ... taught as one who had authority... **99**
MATTHEW 7:28–29

There are three main ways to sum up the Sermon on the Mount:

1. A call to repentance

2. Jesus setting out who he is

3. We recognise that we can't live like this without the help of the Spirit

BUILDING A SECURE FUTURE

ONCLUSION

If you ask, God will give you the **Holy Spirit**.

We need Jesus himself to **come and live within us** to enable us to put this into practice.

NOTES

DISCUSSION QUESTIONS

1. What does it mean to put the words of Jesus into practice? Do you feel that you already do this? If so, how? If not, how can you start?

2. Why does Jesus say that we are in control of what our future holds? Discuss what it means to have a secure future.

3. What is Jesus referring to when he talks about 'houses'? What can we do to ensure they remain strong when they are exposed to the eroding forces around us (see Matthew 7:25)?

4. What are the similarities and differences between the two builders in Jesus' story? How do these relate to life today?

5. How can we be sure that we are followers, and not just admirers of Jesus?